Original title:
The Fish's Voice

Copyright © 2025 Creative Arts Management OÜ
All rights reserved.

Author: Natalia Harrington
ISBN HARDBACK: 978-1-80587-403-4
ISBN PAPERBACK: 978-1-80587-873-5

Tides of Thought

In the depths, a flounder sings,
With bubbles rising, joy it brings.
A school of thoughts, they swim in place,
Chasing dreams with silly grace.

A crab joins in with clacking sounds,
While seaweed sways and spins around.
They dance in circles, swirling light,
Making waves in pure delight.

Riptide Reveries

A dolphin jests, a wave of laughs,
Telling tales of ocean paths.
Each splash a giggle, each roll a jest,
In currents swift, they find their rest.

An octopus with ink in air,
Draws funny faces everywhere.
With every inkblot, stories bloom,
An underwater comical room.

Chants of the Coral

Coral reefs hum a cheeky tune,
With clownfish winking 'neath the moon.
They bubble tunes of bright delight,
With echoes soft, in the pale night.

A starfish giggles, tickles abloom,
As jellyfish dance in a trance of gloom.
In their sea of laughter, all unite,
For a whimsical, underwater night.

The Unseen Symphony

A hidden choir sings down low,
Between the rocks, where currents flow.
They giggle softly, try to tease,
With tickling waves that swirl like breeze.

Anemones sway with playful glee,
Tickling shells, a sight to see.
In murky depths, humor spreads,
Where light meets laughter, joy ahead.

Whirlpools of Wisdom

In bubbly depths, where bubbles play,
A clever trout made quite the display.
He said, "Why swim when you can float?"
All the minnows listened, taking note.

A pufferfish chimed in with a grin,
"Let's play tag, but don't let me win!"
The crowd erupted in splashy glee,
As wisdom whirled in the deep blue sea.

Dreaming in Dorsal

A sardine dreamed of life in a bowl,
With snacks and pool toys, oh what a goal!
"No predators here, just sunlight beams,
I'll be the king of my watery dreams!"

A shark swam by, laughing too loud,
"You dream too big, you silly crowd!"
With fins a-flap and tails a-swish,
They flipped and flopped, diving for fish.

Beneath the Surface Statements

A grouper proclaimed from under a rock,
"Life's like a seaweed, it can't be docked!"
A clam replied, "And don't you forget,
Count your pearls, the best you can get!"

An octopus winked, arms all a-twirl,
"I see more than one side in this whirl!"
All gathered round for a round of cheer,
Making profound statements as only fish leer.

The Flowing Dialogue

In currents swift, the banter flowed,
A clownfish cracked jokes on the road.
"Why did the anemone blush in the tide?"
"Because it saw all those fish slide!"

A snapper replied with a clever quip,
"That's a line I need on my next trip!"
Fishy laughter echoed, through the deep tide,
Where wit and whimsy forever abide.

Secrets of the Algae

In murky green, secrets thrive,
Bubble and swirl, they come alive.
With giggles low, they plot and scheme,
Life beneath, a silly dream.

They whisper tales of guppy pranks,
Dance in currents, avoid the tanks.
Swirling secrets, they giggle and tease,
Underwater jesters with such ease.

Sonata of the Silvery Surface

A silver splash, a tricky swirl,
With fins that flutter and tails that twirl.
They play a tune in bubbly waves,
And hide away in watery caves.

A splashy note, a finned ballet,
They twine and twist in a fishy play.
The concert hall? A mossy stone,
Where underwater giggles are clearly shown.

Watersong of Wonder

In rippling rills, a story flows,
Bubbles dance with cheerful prose.
With each flip, they scribe a line,
In watery worlds, where all's divine.

The clams clap shells, the crab does cheer,
As fishy tales fill the water's sphere.
A concert for gills, it's all a joke,
As laughter floats, and silence folks.

A Mirage of Melodies

In shimmering dreams, tunes drift around,
With seaweed whispers, they can astound.
A playful wink with a swish and sway,
Where bubbles burst in a grand ballet.

The jelly sings and the shrimp does dance,
Life in the deep, a quirky romance.
With melodies that ripple and flow,
A joyous spectacle, come and see the show!

Soundscapes of Silent Streams

In the creek where bubbles sing,
The bubbles giggle, the willows swing.
A gurgling joke from the water's flow,
As minnows tease with their finny show.

A splash and a splash, oh what a scene,
The turtles chuckle, all dressed in green.
They hold their breath for a moment or two,
Then burst into laughter, it's all quite the view.

Languid Cadences of the River

A catfish whispers, 'It's getting late!'
As snails slow dance, 'Oh, isn't it great?'
In rippled laughter, the otters dive,
Each splash a giggle, keeping it alive.

The turtles bob in their lazy parade,
While minnows play hide and seek in the shade.
'Round and 'round, they twirl and they spin,
Creating a ruckus beneath the fin.

The Call of the Companions

Bubbles bubble, gather 'round,
Fishy friends in laughter are found.
They choreograph skits by the reeds,
Under the surface, where humor breeds.

A decisive flip, a playful nudge,
The pikes pretend, just to judge.
'How fast can you swim?' asks the bass with a grin,
While guppies join in, determined to win.

Sonnet of the Stream

Oh, the stream bends with laughter so clear,
Each ripple dances, pulling us near.
A trout sings a tune, quite out of key,
Amusing the frogs, who croak in glee.

An eel does a jig, with quite the flair,
While minnows scatter without a care.
The bubbles conspire, plotting their fun,
In a world where the antics are never quite done.

Underwater Reveries

In a kelp forest, a crab can dance,
With sideways moves, they take a chance,
A clam sings out, a funny tone,
Echoes in currents, slightly overblown.

A dolphin giggles, flips with flair,
Tickles the seaweed, without a care,
A starfish claps, though it has no hands,
Throwing sea parties on whimsical sands.

S underwater Sagas

A pufferfish puffs, with cheeks so wide,
Says, "I'm a balloon! Come take a ride!"
A plucky little shrimp with a grand old tale,
Claims he once rode on a giant whale.

Turtles giggle at the clownfish plight,
Trying to dance, but they just can't get right,
Coral reefs chuckle at the goggle-eyed,
Who think they're mermaids—oh, how they glide!

Waterscape Whimsy

In the bubble blast of the ocean floor,
A wise old octopus tells tales galore,
He twirls his arms, each story a swirl,
Of fish who think they're the favorite pearl.

Sardines gather in a shimmering crowd,
Dancing in circles—oh, they're so proud!
A sea cucumber rolls and gets a cheer,
'Cause his slow salsa brings laughter near.

Secrets from the Shoals

A shrimp in a shell with a top hat on,
Says, "Why wear pants? Come laugh until dawn!"
Fish joke around, with a wink and a nod,
Sharing old secrets of mermaids they prod.

Anemones giggle, tickling small fins,
As jellyfish jive, while chaos begins,
Oh, what a sight from the shoals we adore,
Silly saltwater banter, who could ask for more?

Messages from the Abyss

In the deep where bubble blips,
I heard a tale from guppy quips.
They chat of snacks and seaweed dreams,
While plotting pranks on drifting teams.

A starfish rolls its eyes in jest,
As clams all giggle in their nest.
Whispers float on currents bright,
Making waves with giddy delight.

An octopus dons a silly hat,
While fishy friends all have a chat.
They laugh at crabs that scuttle by,
Swapping tales of every tide.

With gurgles, bubbles, and a splash,
Their wit flows like a playful sash.
At dusk, they dance, a watery show,
Sending giggles in the undertow.

Soft Sounds of the Shoal

In a school of wriggles and swirls,
A trout shares jokes with all the girls.
They squabble softly, flip their tails,
While counting all the jelly trails.

A puffer fish starts to puff and snort,
While clownfish giggle in retort.
They tease the shrimp, both small and bold,
As tales of treasure quests unfold.

Sardines rush in for a comment free,
Singing songs of old sea spree.
The bubble net's a comedy stage,
With laughter bursting from every page.

Beneath the tides, they harmonize,
With funny stories, oh what a prize!
Swishing fins in giggly glee,
The shoal's a riot, can't you see?

The Ocean's Lullaby

In the bays where sea foam plays,
A seahorse croons in funny ways.
With sloshy tunes, the waves join in,
As dolphins dance with cheeky fins.

Anemones giggle, swaying slow,
While starfish tap to the rhythm flow.
The sea turtles chuckle, feeling bright,
As they glide home in the pale moonlight.

With playful splashes, the minnows sway,
Making ripples at the end of day.
They sing of dreams from beneath the blue,
Of silly escapes and oceanic view.

And as the sun bids soft goodbye,
The sea hums sweetly, a giggling cry.
In every ripple, a snicker hides,
The lullaby flows where silliness glides.

Currents of Conversation

Beneath the waves, where currents flow,
The fish all gather, putting on a show.
"Did you hear 'bout the crab with no feet?
He's still the best dancer, can't be beat!"

The stingrays glide with a wink and a tease,
"Watch out for the shipwrecks; it's a breeze!"
With swirling tales and humorous flares,
They huddle tight, sharing their prayers.

The catfish tell tales to the sea anemone,
Inciting laughs in the depths of their harmony.
'Round a coral reef, they spill their beans,
Making waves with their funny routines.

And as the tide brings the night on near,
Their laughter echoes, crisp and clear.
Amidst the seaweed, joy takes flight,
In currents of chatter till morning light.

Psalms of the Plankton

In a world where bubbles rise,
Tiny critters sing their lies.
"Oh, I'm the fastest in the sea!"
While floating strangely, just like me.

With a dance that's quite absurd,
They twirl around without a word.
"Catch me, catch me!" they decree,
While dodging currents, light and free.

They speak in tongues of gurgling glee,
While munching on a zooplankton spree.
Laughing as they tumble and spin,
In the watery depths, they win!

So if you listen, hear their cheer,
A symphony for all to hear.
Plankton pals in a watery rhyme,
Always having a silly time!

The River's Resonance

Once a fish thought it could chime,
With bubbles, bubbles—what a crime!
Said, "I'm the bard of this cool stream!"
Yet splashed about like a bad dream.

With each splash, a fishy tune,
Swooshing past beneath the moon.
"I'm a tenor, can't you see?"
But all that's heard's the sound of pee!

He swayed as currents played their part,
Trying hard to warm the heart.
"Join my band, oh little snail,"
But ended up with tiny ale.

As ripples echoed, what a show,
More laughter than he'd ever know.
Each little wave a giggling mate,
This shard of humor, quite first-rate!

Liquid Lullabies

A turtle crooned a watery tale,
Of a seahorse on a snail trail.
With a wink, he hummed a song,
That went on forever, oh so long!

A fish chimed in, quite off the note,
Belting tunes from his little boat.
"Oh, sweet seaweed, what's today?"
But forgot the lyrics halfway play!

A crab beat time on a hollow shell,
Just swaying wildly, oh so well.
"Come join the show!" he cried aloud,
To all the fishes in a crowd.

So under waves, it's quite absurd,
As silence breaks with chuckles heard.
Liquid laughter fills the brine,
Where every note is perfectly fine!

Gurgles of the Grotto

In a spooky cave, fish tales unwind,
Where secrets bubble in the blind.
With gurgles loud, they start to plot,
A funny scheme that means a lot.

"Let's throw a party," one fish said,
With glowing bulbs that floated ahead.
"We'll feast on plankton, dance all night,
With jellyfish lanterns shining bright!"

As shadows flickered on the walls,
They wiggled, squiggled, having ball.
But suddenly, the currents swayed,
And turned their dance into a parade!

So watch the grotto fill with cheer,
As underwater friends draw near.
Each gurgle turns to laughter now,
As fish join in—oh, take a bow!

Hushed Harmonies of the Lagoon

In waters deep, where secrets swim,
A fish with dreams starts to grin.
It wiggles and jigs, a comical sight,
Chasing its tail in pure delight.

The turtles laugh, the crabs tap toes,
While bubbles rise, as laughter flows.
"Who knew," they say, "that fins could sing?"
In joyful tones, they dance and swing.

With every splash, a giggle bursts,
As happy fish quench bubble thirsts.
They form a band, a quirky show,
In the quiet lagoon, oh how they glow.

So join the crowd, just give a cheer,
For every fish's tune you hear.
In this funny world beneath the sea,
Laughter is the key; it's so carefree!

The Echoing Fin

Swishing and swashing, the fins collide,
Making a ruckus in playful pride.
They send out sounds like silly peeps,
While seaweed giggles and softly creeps.

Oh, one fish croaked a tune so wrong,
Echoing back, it was quite strong.
The dolphins joined, in a jazzy mess,
Fins flailing about, what a funny stress!

Then came a starfish with sticky feet,
Adding a rhythm that was hard to beat.
Poking and prodding the fish around,
It turned the whole show into a clown-bound.

When the waves settled, their sides would ache,
From laughter shared, the smiles not fake.
In the echoing depths, they'd sing and spin,
What a wild time with the echoing fin!

Secrets Told in Bubbles

In glittering waters, bubbles rise,
Whispering secrets in crafty ties.
A fish spins tales of wiggly bliss,
As bubbles dance and giggle with a hiss.

"Oh, did you hear about Sammy Squid?
He tried to hide but the bubbles slid!
They floated out, where all could see,
His silly face, oh what a spree!"

Each bubble popped with laughter loud,
As fish gathered round, a curious crowd.
"Tell us more," they said with glee,
Spin another tale, just wait and see!

With frothy whispers, the stories poured,
Of silly pranks that their friends adored.
In the world where nothing's subtle,
Secrets told in bubbles, endless chuckles!

Lullabies of the Lagoon

As night descends, the lagoon glows soft,
With a lullaby whispered, cozy aloft.
Fish drift to sleep on sparkly beds,
Dreaming of laughter, with silly spreads.

A clownfish hums, a tune so bright,
While the shrimp tap dance, a funny sight.
"Close your eyes, the night is here,
Let the lullabies bring you cheer!"

Moonlight shimmers, casting a spell,
As fishy friends gather, all under the shell.
Chit-chatting quietly, they share their dreams,
Lullabies floating like soft, gentle streams.

So cuddle tight in the lagoon's embrace,
Where even little fish find their place.
With smiles and giggles, they peacefully float,
Dreaming sweet dreams in a friend-filled boat!

The Quietest Song

Bubbles rise, a silent tune,
Swishing fins beneath the moon.
Giggling scales in water's sway,
Whispers heard from far away.

Guppies laugh, a splashy jest,
Dancing in their tiny vest.
Neon dreams in currents swirl,
As laughter ripples, bright and twirl.

A snail hums, unsure of pitch,
While minnows tease, they flip and twitch.
Tiny hearts beat out of tune,
In the ocean's soft cocoon.

So let the waters sing their cheer,
In gurgles grand, we have no fear.
For every silence has a rhyme,
Where fish and dreams combine in time.

Rhythms of the Riverbed

In the shallows, a grouchy trout,
Makes a fuss with a mighty shout.
Silly rocks just roll their eyes,
As he flounders and softly sighs.

Crabs in rhythm, tap a beat,
While minnows wiggle, oh so neat.
Currents carry the glee around,
In this dance upon the ground.

The catfish grins, a oily smile,
Swishing through the water's aisle.
"Can we tune this party up?"
He yelps with joy, a bubbly sup.

They spin and twirl, a quirky band,
With bubbles popping, oh so grand.
In this crazy underwater shindig,
The riverbed's a dancing gig.

Conversations with Currents

Two goldfish chat in flowing streams,
About their wildest, wettest dreams.
"One day I'll swim to the big blue sea!"
"Now wait a minute, what about me?"

A catfish grumbles, "Let's be clear,
My cousin's hooked, he's gone from here!"
"I'd rather float than take a chance,"
Said the goldfish, with a wiggle dance.

Turtles nod in wise old jest,
As they ponder who's the best.
"Let's plan a race, surely it's time!"
"Slow and steady," croaks the slime.

Amidst the bubbles, laughter swells,
Stories told, in watery wells.
In the giggles of the stream so bright,
Every creature finds delight.

Tales from the Tidal Pool

In the tidal pool, a sea star reads,
A book of jokes, for silly needs.
The hermit crab chuckles, makes a joke,
As the octopus grins and begins to poke.

"Why do clams never share their pearls?
Because they love to keep their swirls!"
Pufferfish giggles, rolls about,
While seaweed sways with a silly shout.

Anemones sway, playing tag,
While starfish join with a carefree wag.
"Catch me if you can," they sing,
As crabs in style take on the fling.

Every tide tells a tale anew,
Where laughter bubbles and friendships brew.
In the shallows where fun meets the shore,
Tidal tales shared forevermore.

The Silent Call of the Sea

A sea without a sound, a bubbling laugh,
A dolphin trying hard to draw a graph.
The waves whisper secrets, but fish just grin,
Their silence is loud, a mischievous sin.

With barnacles tapping on shells all around,
They dance and they twirl, making giggles abound.
An octopus juggles, quite a funny sight,
While seaweed joins in, swaying left and right.

A crab scuttles by in a silly parade,
With a clumsy little step, never dismayed.
The currents hum softly, a tickling cheer,
As fish tell bad jokes that only they hear.

So down in the deep, where the laughter won't cease,
The creatures compete for a moment of peace.
Bubbles arise from a flirtatious prance,
The silent sea giggles—oh, what a chance!

Melodies of the Marine

Bubbles pop like popcorn in a comical show,
As the clownfish giggles, putting on a glow.
A whale hums a ditty, all wobbly and round,
While seahorses two-step, hips moving astound.

Starfish croak jokes with their five-pointed wit,
As dolphins sing loudly, each note a bit lit.
Plankton throw parties, with twinkles and lights,
While mermaids dance wildly on moonlight nights.

A grouper struts by, wearing sunglasses cool,
With a swagger so silly, it's breaking all rules.
"Why did the coral cross the ocean floor?"
"To get to the reef side! Now who wants some more?"

So take a deep dive, let your laughter take flight,
In waters where tunes make the day feel just right.
Each splash is a giggle, a song on repeat,
Where everyone's jiving, life's pretty sweet!

Lurking Lyricism

In shadows of kelp where the weird fish reside,
They murmur and chatter, their moods runneth wide.
A pufferfish puffing, looking awfully proud,
Tells puns to the crabs, drawing quite the crowd.

An anglerfish glimmers, a spotlighted act,
"Why don't fish play cards?" Well, that's a good fact!
"Too many sharks around, they'll take all the stakes!"
The sea chuckles softly, it's all about breaks.

Jellyfish jelly, waving without a care,
They jive to the rhythm of waves in the air.
A parrotfish squirts ink, as it bursts into song,
Helping everyone laugh, the ocean's where they belong.

So lurk in the depths where the laughter is sly,
Every hiccup a symphony, swirling nearby.
In currents of whimsy, let giggles encore,
For the waters are filled with a lyrical score!

Arcane Anemone Anthems

Beneath swirling currents where the odd ones convene,
The anemones wiggle in a whimsical scene.
"Why do we dive?" asks a clownfish with flair,
"To catch all the best jokes that swim in the air!"

Tentacles dancing in a joyful parade,
As fish form a choir, their voices displayed.
They harmonize blends of the goofiest tunes,
While bubble rings float like brightly lit moons.

Anemones giggle, their tentacles sway,
As they echo the laughter that bubbles all day.
"Here's a riddle," they chant, "What's slippery, slick?
A fish riding waves with an old rubber stick!"

So cherish the magic beneath rippling waves,
Where the anemones sing, and the sea always braves.
In ocean's embrace, where the fun never ends,
Life swims with the silly, and laughter transcends!

Song of the Silent Waters

In bubbles, secrets float and dance,
The minnows hum a cheeky prance.
Tales of splashes, fishy laughs,
In watery worlds, the humor crafts.

Gilly giggles from beneath the waves,
As tangly seaweed quietly braves.
Fins flapping to an unseen beat,
The ocean's jesters, oh, what a treat!

Crabs in costumes, a shellfish show,
Jellyfish jiggle, putting on a glow.
With swishy tails, they throw a ball,
In the silent waters, laughter calls.

Beneath the Surface Lullaby

In dreamy depths, where shadows play,
The guppies giggle at the end of the day.
Each ticklish current sings a tune,
A light-hearted serenade under the moon.

Starfish stick, but never quite stay,
With a wiggly dance, they slip away.
Octopus antics, full of surprise,
Mimicking humans with winking eyes.

The snappy shrimp with chatter so quick,
Offers a joke with every flick.
Peculiar sounds from bubbles they make,
In this funny realm, no one is fake.

Choreography of Fins

In the school of fish, they form a line,
With flutters and flips, their steps align.
They twirl and whirl in a sea parade,
A dance of the fins, oh, what a charade!

Clownfish chuckle, the star of the show,
While grumpy flatfish lie down low.
The anglerfish grins with a light so bright,
As they all groove through the jelly moonlight.

What a sight, this underwater ball,
With bubbles floating, they heed the call.
A choreographed splash, a twist and a slide,
In this funny ballet, their joy won't hide.

Gossamer Secrets of the Sea

Whispers of ripples, so soft and sly,
Where the seaweed dances and the seahorses fly.
Ticklish tides tell tales of fun,
In a giggling current, forever they run.

Lobsters in top hats, what a strange sight,
Tapping their claws in the soft moonlight.
The hermit crab struts in an old boot,
Stealing the scene in his quirky suit.

With stories of fish that swim out of line,
Creating a ruckus, one fin at a time.
Under this surface, laughter's a game,
Gossamer secrets, we never name.

The Quiet Chorus

In waters deep, they sing so fine,
Sardines in sequins, paired with brine.
Clownfish giggle, what a sight,
While crabs hold concerts, what a fright!

They croon in bubbles, quite a tune,
Turtles sway, in a dance with the moon.
Octopi juggle, to laughs we cheer,
An underwater cabaret, oh dear!

Each note they share, a water ballet,
Flipping through verses, in their own way.
With seaweed jazz and coral rock,
This underwater crew, always a shock!

So if you dive and hear them play,
Join the fun, don't drift away.
For down below, laughter's abound,
In the depths, joy's always found!

Below the Waves' Whispers

Where bubbles rise, and laughter's clear,
Fish trade stories, no need to leer.
A whale tells jokes, with a booming voice,
While anemones sway, they all rejoice.

Seahorses trot, wearing tiny frowns,
Making faces, avoiding crowns.
The grouper grins, with a cheeky flip,
As clownfish giggle on a light-hearted trip.

With shrimp that dance in humorous strides,
The jellyfish twirl, amusement abides.
Tiny snails slow dance, without a care,
Under currents that pull, they sway in the air.

Listen closely, you might just hear,
Guffaws and chortles, drawing near.
In the deep blue, laughter's the game,
Creating joy, it's never the same!

Whispers Beneath the Waves

Beneath the surface, secrets sail,
With funny tales that never fail.
Angelfish gossip, share some glee,
While pufferfish puff in sheer esprit.

A turtle chuckles, as he glides,
While sardines swirl, in playful tides.
They whisper jokes in tones so light,
As rays surf through with pure delight.

Giggling grunts create a scene,
Witty remarks traded in between.
Starfish spread jokes like rays of sun,
In this watery realm, there's never 'done'.

So come enjoy this fishy jest,
In ocean depths, with laughter blessed.
Where bubbles burst and humor flows,
Beneath the waves, anything goes!

Echoes of the Deep Blue

In the great blue, echo a laugh,
Mackerels swim, plotting their path.
With each ripple, a punchline waits,
Bubbles tickle, surprise awaits!

A dolphin sneezes, causing a splash,
While tuna schools in a colorful clash.
With sea cucumbers, who don't find it fair,
Turned into a joke, with flair in the air.

Laughter dances on waves that rise,
A shark tells tales, quite a surprise.
As jellyfish sway, doing their best,
In this watery stage, there's humor, a fest!

So dive on down and share a grin,
Join the fun where the chuckles begin.
Below the surface, joy's in the hue,
Where echoes of laughter carry through!

Chorus of the Clear Waters

In the pond where splashes reign,
Frogs croak out a silly refrain.
A carp with dreams of singing glory,
Tells tales that swim in watery story.

Bubbles dance in a bubbly show,
As minnows hum in a row.
The turtles join with comical clicks,
Making waves with their funny tricks.

Sunfish strut like they own the place,
Each wiggle flaunts a fishy grace.
In gurgling giggles, the eels entwine,
While catfish grin with a grand design.

A finned sensation in every dive,
In this laughter, the pond's alive!
With echoes of joy and splashes bold,
This aquatic jest will never grow old.

The Aquatic Aria

A bubble blew a mighty tune,
As dolphins danced beneath the moon.
With sprightly flips and joyous leaps,
They share secrets that the current keeps.

The octopus dons a bowtie flair,
While clownfish giggle, unaware.
Krill applaud with tiny hands,
In this underwater rock band.

Seaweed sways in rhythm tight,
As angelfish add a pop of light.
Every ripple's a note in the swell,
A joyful concert in their shell.

From coral stages, the laughter springs,
As ocean critters serenade with wings.
With smiles and splashes all around,
This quirky aria knows no bound.

In the Embrace of Eddies

Round and round in a playful whirl,
Where the minnows twist, dance, and twirl.
With giggles flying, currents sway,
As the riverbank cheers their ballet.

A catfish sways with a silly grin,
While a tadpole dreams of the grand swim-in.
Through bubbles, voices rise and fall,
Echoing laughter in the watery hall.

The heron chuckles low from the shore,
As trout tell jokes and beg for more.
In playful splashes, the fun persists,
As the river plots its whimsical twists.

Eddies spin tales as they whiz by,
Beneath the sun and the vast blue sky.
In this merry dance of feather and fin,
Every laugh is a joyful win.

Voices from the Abyss

In the deep where shadows play,
With sea monsters that joke away.
A squid throws shade with tentacle flair,
While a grouper grunts, 'We don't care!'

The clams all hush, their shells closed tight,
As anemones wiggle in sheer delight.
With playful jabs from pufferfish bold,
And a lobster who tells tales of old.

The jellyfish glow like lanterns bright,
As they float and drift without a fright.
Echoes bounce with bubbly joy,
In this abyss, laughter's the ploy.

Conversations of bubbles and drifts ensue,
Where the curious gather to hear what's new.
From depths profound, a chortle breaks free,
As the ocean laughs along with glee.

An Ode to Oceanic Dreamers

Bubbles burst with laugh and cheer,
Grouchy crab grumbles, yet draws near.
Seahorses gossip, tales to share,
In a swirl of fun, they float in air.

Jellyfish jiggle, a jolly spree,
Clownfish chuckle, as bright as can be.
Starfish salute with a stiffened wave,
While the octopus makes a fashion save.

Turtles tell tales of slothful lore,
While the anglerfish just wants to score.
The reef's a stage where all can play,
In aquatic silliness, they sway away.

So raise a toast to the sea's fine jest,
Where each little critter puts humor to test.
In the depths where the waves make a fuss,
Life's a funny tale, come join the bus!

Muffled Echoes of Exploration

In the depths where giggles dwell,
Fishy friends weave tales to tell.
Echoes giggle with a playful tone,
As bubbles whisper secrets known.

Anemones chuckle, tickle the sand,
While lobsters dance in a crazy band.
The hermit crab jokes, 'I'm not so shy,'
With a shell too big, it's hard to lie.

Dolphins play peek-a-boo with the sun,
Surprising swimmers, oh what fun!
They flip and twirl, adding to the mirth,
In this splashy world, laughter's the worth.

The seaweed sways, joins in the play,
As creatures frolic, come what may.
With each bubbling note, the ocean's voice,
Rings out with joy, oh what a choice!

Dances of Silent Shadows

Beneath the waves, shadows unite,
Witty whispers in the soft twilight.
Eels do the cha-cha, what a sight,
While clams groove by in purely delight.

Squid swirl and twirl, ink clouds around,
While the anemone sways without a sound.
The pufferfish puffs, feeling so spry,
It's a silent party, oh my oh my!

The flounder hides, but can't miss the beat,
With a shuffle and slide, it's quick on its feet.
Creatures in darkness, moving with glee,
In the hush of the ocean, they dance wild and free.

So join in the fun where light meets shade,
With each secret step, the waves cascade.
In this watery ballroom, laughter prevails,
As shadows skitter, dancing the tales.

Voices in the Stillness

In quiet waters, giggles arise,
Lobsters whisper, plotting surprise.
Corals snicker as tides come and go,
A stillness that teases with humor's glow.

The turtles chuckle, 'Let's race to the shell!'
With slow-motion speed, they glide quite well.
Fish parade in colors that tickle the eye,
Creating a scene that makes sand castles fly.

Bubbles murmur, jokes pop like fizz,
While sea slugs wonder, 'What is this whizz?'
In the serene depths, laughter does bloom,
As the ocean chuckles, commanding the room.

So listen close, in the calm of the sea,
With shy little voices as funny as can be.
In the stillness of waves where creatures rejoice,
Echoes of laughter, the ocean's sweet voice.

Tides of Tranquility

Splish-splash, they dance and play,
Little scales in the sun's warm ray.
Bubbles giggle as they float,
In a watery world, they all gloat.

Gazing up through the waves so bright,
Fishy friends laugh with sheer delight.
With every flip and every swirl,
They share secrets in a whirl.

In the coral, a party starts,
With seaweed snacks and jelly tarts.
They wiggle and waggle, what a sight,
Creating ripples that burst with light.

When the tides give a cheeky grin,
Fishy tales of mischief begin.
They orchestrate their ocean joke,
As giggling bubbles rise and choke.

Reflections of Whispered Wisdom

In the deep, where the giggles grow,
A sage fish whispers to and fro.
"Don't be shy, come out and play,
The current's fine, hip-hip hooray!"

With brightly colored scales of flair,
They swim through swirls of salt-kissed air.
One wears glasses, the wise old trout,
"Life's a jest, so let it out!"

They gather 'round a quirky shell,
Sharing giggles, oh what a spell!
"If you can't swim, just float and dream,
Catch the wave, ride the gleam!"

And as the stars reflect and dance,
They twirl and tumble in a trance.
Laughter echoes from fin to fin,
A symphony where all can win.

Twilight Tales of the Tide

Under moonlight's gentle sway,
The water's alive, night meets day.
Fish flip and flop with a wink,
Spilling stories quicker than you think.

A dreamy eel, with a clever jest,
Announces a fishy talent quest.
"Can you dance? Can you sing?
Show your moves, let your fun take wing!"

They splash like stars in the inky sky,
Hooting and hollering as they fly.
With every twirl and every dive,
They remind us all, oh how to thrive.

The tide chuckles, the sea laughs too,
It's a fishy frolic; what more to do?
With jokes and stunts by moonlit beams,
They weave together their silly dreams.

Abyssal Lullabies

In the depths where shadows creep,
Silent fish sing songs to sleep.
With a flick of fin and a giggly tail,
They rock and roll in a coral sail.

At ocean's bottom, an octopus croons,
Bubbles dance to the melody of tunes.
"Let's tell tales of treasure lost,
And laughter found in storms we tossed!"

A clownfish joins with a vibrant cheer,
With silly faces, they banter near.
Jellyfish sway like lanterns bright,
Guiding their pals through the whimsical night.

In their lullabies, the punchlines rise,
Making starlit waves laugh and sigh.
As the currents cradle them, soft and light,
They drift away into dreams so bright.

Chants of the Estuary

In the reeds where the giggles swim,
Frog has started a karaoke hymn.
With a splash and a flip, they all join in,
Harmonizing like a merry fish kin.

Crabs dance sideways, clapping their claws,
Twirling around, they ignore the laws.
Gulls squawk and chirp, trying to sing,
Creating chaos, a real comedy fling.

The turtles chuckle, necks all stretched wide,
As the minnows perform with sheer bubbly pride.
Who knew that the pond could hold such a show?
Life below the surface, a grand cabaret glow!

So gather your friends and come take a peek,
Where laughter and splashes turn water to cheek.
In this vivacious estuary delight,
Every bubble is bursting with joy and pure light.

Whispers from the Watershed

Bubbles bubbling with secrets untold,
In the creek where the sprightly fish scold.
"I swear I saw a worm wearing a hat!"
The gossip spreads like a friendly spat.

Little guppies prance, their tails in a swirl,
While an octopus dreams of a dance with a girl.
"Two left feet!" they giggle, "What a sight!"
As they twirl and twist under moonbeam light!

Perch are plotting a splashy surprise,
With cod on the side, they're wise and quite spry.
Together they whisper in currents they know,
Jokes that ripple and flow like a show.

As tadpoles chuckle, they weave through the rush,
Inventing new games during a drenched hush.
In the chatty waterways where wit flows free,
Every splash is a punchline, a loud jubilee!

Aquarium of Ancient Echoes

In a tank where old tales swim with flair,
Goldfish gossip without a single care.
"Remember the time we snuck out at night?"
"Oh please, that's a story, but I'll take your bite!"

The lobster laughs, his claws raised in jest,
"Dance like a shrimp, now that's quite the test!"
Stars and stripes on the fish made of dreams,
All share their tales like whimsical themes.

A pufferfish bloats, proclaims he's a star,
"I'm the best singer, by far, oh so bizarre!"
While the angelfish blush at his bold serenade,
Reef tales unfold in a colorful parade.

With bubbles of laughter and winked little eyes,
The secrets of water become their surprise.
In an aquarium where echoes are fun,
Every splash spins a story, a laughter run!

Flowing Fragments of Fables

Down by the stream, where the chatter is light,
Trout tell tall tales, both funny and bright.
"Once I leaped higher than the great kingfisher!"
The crowd laughs and titter at his tongue-in-cheek swisher.

Snails in their shells spin yarns of their quests,
"Just yesterday, I raced with the best!"
"Your shell's a racetrack?" the creek critters roar,
Belly laughs rippling from the sandy floor.

The wise old catfish, with whiskers so grand,
Shares legends of treasure buried in the sand.
"Diamonds? Nah, just glowworms in a feast!"
Giggles erupt, echoing their joy at least!

Grins gild the waters where fables take flight,
Fishy friends gathered, sharing laughs in the night.
In flowing fragments, the stories ignite,
Creating a mosaic of humor's pure light.

Symphony of Silent Swimmers

In waters deep, they glide with grace,
Little fins flapping, each in their place.
They whisper jokes in secret tones,
While seaweed giggles, the coral moans.

A clownfish laughs at a lobster's plight,
Says, "You're not funny, but you sure are bright!"
The octopus dances, an oceanic jest,
While turtles nod, feeling quite blessed.

The dolphins chuckle in synchronized play,
As anchovies twirl, not knowing the way.
With bubbles and blunders, the sea critters cheer,
Creating a symphony that no one can hear.

Underwater antics, a hilarious scene,
Where fish wear top hats and occasionally preen.
As tides ebb and flow, the laughter rolls by,
In a world beneath waves, where humor won't die.

Unsung Melodies of the Ocean

A tuna rehearses its solo tonight,
But gets stage fright and swims out of sight.
Crab's in the back, holding its claws tight,
While a starfish concedes—it can't sing, that's right!

The seahorse strums on a seaweed guitar,
Every note floats up, oh, so bizarre!
With a wink and a splash, it plays out of key,
Even the jellyfish groove—oh, what a spree!

The waves may not carry their tunes to the shore,
But fish throw a party, and who could ask for more?
While the sun sets low, the barnacles grin,
At the unsung melodies bubbling within.

So if you're near water, don't take it in vain,
Listen close, you might hear the ocean's refrain.
Even in silence, the laughter won't cease,
As they jam under currents, a true underwater feast.

Cod's Confession

In the murky depths, a cod took a stand,
With a microphone made from driftwood and sand.
"I've got secrets, oh yes, quite a tale,
Of love, and loss, and a very small snail!"

The audience gathered—shrimps, crabs, and more,
Each one intrigued by the tales from the floor.
With every odd story, the sea started to roll,
As eels couldn't help but crack up and console.

"My crush on a flounder, it was such a big deal,
But turns out, she preferred her next meal!"
The crowd burst with laughter, a raucous delight,
As cod found its rhythm and soared through the night.

So if you think fish just swim without glee,
Remember the cod and its stand-up spree.
For deep in the sea, where the silliness flows,
Even the shyest have stories to expose.

The Language of Gills

In the sea where whispers float like foam,
Gills converse in water, far from home.
With blinks and bubbles, they share their tales,
Of missing a meal or escaping the gales.

A winking angelfish joins the parade,
While a pouty puffer shows off its shade.
"I can puff up, but really, I won't!"
Says a sardine, with a comical flaunt.

The clownfish gesticulates wildly with flair,
While anemones roll their eyes in despair.
"Just face the sea currents, don't overreact!"
And the sea cucumbers nod to the pact.

With giggles and gurgles, the gills keep it light,
In this underwater world of sheer delight.
So listen real close, for the fun that abounds,
In the language of gills, laughter resounds!

Whispers of the Wetlands

In the murky muck, tales are spun,
A soggy singer, just for fun.
Bubbles pop with a squeaky cheer,
Giggling reeds, lend us your ear!

A frog in shades, croaking with glee,
Chorusing tunes from the evergreen spree.
The dragonflies dance to a slippery beat,
While turtles roll in rhythm, oh what a feat!

Tiny fish quack in sparkly jest,
Chasing down laughter, they're truly blessed.
The cattails sway, they bob and weave,
As natural jesters, they never leave!

In the wetlands where giggles roam,
Giggling minnows find their home.
Splash and splatter, wetland flair,
With every chuckle, joy fills the air!

Lament of the Leaping Trout

Out of the water, with a grand leap,
Trout tell tales, while the catfish sleep.
They hurl through air, with a wink and spin,
Splashing down in a bubbly din!

"Hey there, folks, come watch our show,
We flip and flop, putting on a glow!"
With flippers flapping, they aim for the sky,
Making clouds giggle as they fly by!

The river grins under the sunny light,
While otters chuckle at the fishy flight.
They cast a line, yet laughter strikes,
The leaping trout, the true fish mics!

Waving ribbons, they dance with pride,
In a swirl of giggles, they take a ride.
Kissing the breeze, the cool water sings,
A comedic opera, oh what joy it brings!

Translucent Melodies

In crystal pools where chortles play,
The shimmering fish, in joyful array.
Tails like trumpets, they wiggle and sway,
Laughing bubbles keep troubles at bay!

Blowing kisses to the sunny air,
Silly splashes, without a care.
Gleeful gurgles, they hum a tune,
A symphony sung beneath the moon!

With glistening scales, they prance and twirl,
Each flip and flop, makes the water whirl.
Pirouetting fish with a splashy grin,
In the underwater laughter, all joins in!

Underneath the waves, the joke is grand,
Whiskered catfish, lending a hand.
Creating ripples in a shimmering sea,
Where translucent melodies dance so free!

Tones of the Tranquil Tide

Near the gentle shore, the tides do sweep,
Silly sea creatures swirl in a heap.
Seagulls crack jokes, with a flap and a flap,
While fish in formation plan a slapstick map!

"Oh! A splash here, and a swirl there,"
As starfish chuckle without a care.
With barnacles giggling atop their backs,
They tell jokes that lead to more laughs and cracks!

Octopuses juggle with inky flair,
Showing off talents with glittering stare.
A clam in the mix, with a pearl of a pun,
Bringing joy to the tides, where laughter is spun!

Rolling waves carry cheer on high,
Tickling the fins, as they swim by.
Within this playful aquatic scene,
The tones of the tranquil tide reign supreme!

Songs of the Scales

In bubbles they giggle, in currents they glide,
With tales of the ocean, they cannot hide.
A sardine sings sweetly, a mackerel jives,
As seaweed dances, their joy just thrives.

The squids hold a concert, with ink as their art,
While eels do the twist, a slippery start.
Clownfish tell jokes, oh what a delight,
In this deep blue circus, all feels just right.

With a flip of a tail, they start a parade,
Bubbles of laughter, they serenely wade.
A pufferfish pops, with a showman's flair,
In this underwater gig, there's fun everywhere!

So let us join in, both fish and people,
In this joyful splash, where life's never steeple.
With fins in the air, and laughter abound,
In the ocean's own choir, pure joy can be found.

The Language of Fins

A flounder flips funny, a flat little face,
Says, "Come on, swim over, let's quicken the pace!"
With winks from the wrasse, and chirps from the crab,
They share little secrets, no need for a jab.

Tangs talk of fashion, each scale has its style,
While clownfish share puns, they could giggle a while.
The octopi whisper with arms full of flair,
Mimicking motions, it's quite the affair!

From bass with their boisterous, bold bubbling chats,
To sleepy old catfish, who snooze on their mats.
The currents carry laughter, like bubbles they float,
In this grand fin-tastic, fishy old moat.

So listen quite closely, for those in the deep,
With laughter and giggles, they're never asleep.
A chorus of characters, under waves they play,
In the watery kingdom, their antics hold sway.

Underwater Serenade

The dolphins compose with their clicks and their whirls,
As sea turtles groove, giving currents good twirls.
A starfish conducts, with limbs wide and proud,
In this underwater show, they gather a crowd.

The lobsters recite poems in pinchy delight,
While jellyfish glide, a soft glowing sight.
Anemones sway, catching laughs all around,
As seahorses trot, in their prancy bounds.

Bubbles form symphonies, echoing wide,
As the eels pull a prank on the waiters' side.
The shrimp tell stories, all witty and bright,
In this wet wonderland, everything feels right.

With bubbles as beats and seaweed in tune,
The laughter of fish dances under the moon.
So join in the fun, let your spirits take flight,
In the depths of the sea, everything's light.

Harmony of the Hidden Currents

A sneaky old crab, with a grin on his face,
Hides behind a rock, in his clam-shell space.
With whispers he shares, in the dimmest of light,
Stories of tuna and their remarkable flight.

Goldfish in schools, with their synchronized plays,
Doing belly-flops, in hilarious ways.
The pike just smirks, from his shadowy lair,
While minnows play tag, with a splash and a flare.

Grouper regales how he caught the best meal,
While guppies conspire, with dreams that they feel.
A stingray freestyles, gliding slow like a breeze,
In this watery world, laughter huggers with ease.

So let's all unite, in this splashy discourse,
With laughter and giggles, they take their own course.
In the waves of the sea, friendships will flow,
In the harmony hidden, the fun's on the go!

Ripples of Reflection

Bubbles rise like giggles, soft and light,
As fish gossip under the moonlight.
They tell tales of hooks that missed the mark,
And swim in circles, making their spark.

A scale slick as a joke, a flick of the tail,
Echoes of laughter in the wet, cool veil.
With eyes wide as saucers, they spin and glide,
Mimicking mermaids with nothing to hide.

Voices of the Blue

Under the waves where the seaweed sways,
Fish have their meetings with humorous plays.
The clowns wear stripes while the fins do the dance,
Silly antics abound in a watery trance.

Telling tall tales of boats that go by,
With a flip of the fin, they let out a sigh.
Their laughter bubbles up like foam on the tide,
In a comedy show where no one can hide.

The Wordless Waters

In silent currents, where ripples explode,
Fish make a ruckus in their underwater abode.
They splash and they dart like kids in a stream,
Creating a spectacle, living the dream.

Their gills flap and flutter, a whimsical sight,
In a theater of tides, they banter with might.
With no need for words, just a swish and a swirl,
They cast their net wide in a watery whirl.

A Chorus of Gills

In a meadow of kelp, where laughter is ripe,
A chorus of gills brings joy in each pipe.
With a wink and a nod, they perform for the reef,
Their tunes ripple out, bringing bubbles of relief.

Like a jazz band of scales, they play all night,
With echoes of chuckles that dance in the light.
Their shrieks blend with bubbles, a musical hoot,
In the underwater circus, they're ever so cute.

Whispers Beneath the Waves

A flounder flaps, with tales to tell,
Of fishy dreams and a slippery shell.
A tuna giggles, a clownfish grins,
Swapping stories of their aquatic sins.

Bubbles rise like popcorn flies,
As seaweed sways and laughter sighs.
The crabs crack jokes from their sandy lair,
While a hermit crab pretends not to care.

An octopus winks with eight arms in play,
"Who's the best juggler? I'll show you today!"
With a splash and a swirl, the sea turns bright,
As fish don wigs and dance through the night.

A blowfish puffs, "I'm the life of the show!"
And others all chime in, "We love it so!"
With a flip and a flop, they laugh till they ache,
Down by the reef, it's one big fish cake!

Echoes from the Deep

In coral castles, whispers arise,
Clam shells giggle, fish masks disguise.
A dolphin chuckles, orca rhymes,
Underwater antics in slippery climes.

The sardines dance in perfect sync,
A fishy flash mob, oh what a kink!
With a splash and a dash, they twirl and spin,
Each one trying to see who can win.

"Why did the grouper cross the sea?"
"To dive with friends, that's his decree!"
The sea anemone rolls with glee,
As clownfish snicker, "He's so silly!"

Echoes bounce in the turquoise swell,
While jellyfish float in a shimmering spell.
A manta ray glides with elegance supreme,
Living the moment, living the dream!

Secrets of the Silent Stream

In a quiet brook where minnows play,
A tadpole whispers, "My tail's in the way!"
Frogs join in with a croaky croon,
Singing their hearts out to the light of the moon.

Water striders skate on the gleam,
While dragonflies buzz, living the dream.
"Have you heard 'bout the fish with the hat?"
A little guppy chirps, "Now, wasn't that fat?"

A waterfall chuckles, "Oh, what a sight!
Fish with flair, a colorful flight!"
As ripples of laughter ripple and swell,
Where secrets and gags in the water dwell.

"Why don't fish use the computer?" says one,
"They can't get their fins on the keyboard, it's fun!"
So they splash and they giggle all under the sun,
In the silent stream where the hilarity runs!

Murmurs of the Ocean

Whispers ride on the ocean breeze,
Fish trade tales with the swaying trees.
A starfish grins, "What's the best dance?"
As schools of herring sway in a trance.

With every wave, there's giggles galore,
The sea turtle leaps, then crashes ashore.
"Did you hear about the fish in a suit?"
He strutted so fine, till he slipped on his boot!

Anemones blush at the sea urchin's pun,
"Why are we friends? Because you're so fun!"
They dance in the tides as barnacles cheer,
While dolphins compose songs that all fish hear.

"Oh, let's have a show!" sings a clam on the reef,
As sea cucumbers roll—what a goofy belief!
In the murmurs of life, the ocean's alive,
With laughter and stories, they all brightly thrive!

www.ingramcontent.com/pod-product-compliance
Lightning Source LLC
Chambersburg PA
CBHW060142230426
43661CB00003B/529